"WHE'RE YER FOR?"

Published by Chaffcutter Books, 2006
in association with the Society for Sailing Barge Research

ISBN 0 9532422-9-3

Also by Anthony Osler: Introduction to the Probation Service, Waterside Press 1995

THE SOCIETY FOR SAILING BARGE RESEARCH

The Society for Spritsail Barge Research was established in 1963 by a band of enthusiasts concerned that the rapid decline and possible extinction of these splendid and historically significant craft would pass largely unrecorded. From the thousands of Thames sailing barges once plying the estuaries of the south-east and beyond, today just a handful survive in active commission, charter parties and business guests replacing the grain, cement and coal cargoes of yesteryear.

Now renamed The Society for Sailing Barge Research, reflecting a broadening interest in other allied types of craft, the Society organises walks, talks and exhibitions and regularly publishes Topsail, a treasure chest of sailing barge history profusely illustrated with fascinating photographs of long lost craft and the ports they once served. In 2006 the Society established an Archive of sailing barge documents and photographs and is actively acquiring individual items and collections for preservation and study. Members also receive a twice yearly newsletter which highlights the fortunes of those barges which survive, as well as providing further snippits of our maritime heritage as ongoing research yields yet more of that trade, a way of life which from origins going back hundreds, even thousands of years, ceased in 1970 when the *Cambria* carried her last cargo under sail alone. For more information see the Society web site at www.sailingbargeresearch.org.uk.

Membership enquiries to:
Margaret Blackburn,
Lords Bridge Toll House, Lordsbridge, Tilney cum Islington, Kings Lynn, Norfolk PE34 3BW

Chaffcutter Books, 39 Friars Road, Braughing, Ware, Hertfordshire SG11 2NN, England

Printed and bound in Great Britain by Piggott Black Bear Limited, Cambridge CB1 8DH, England

"WHE'RE YER FOR?"

The Recollections of Capt. Harold Smy, Sailing Bargemaster

Text by Anthony Osler

Drawings by Angus Stirling

CHAFFCUTTER

CONTENTS

Anthony Osler was born at Ipswich in 1938 and has had a love of anything that will float ever since his father (who worked for R. & W. Paul, the Ipswich maltsters) started taking him to look around Ipswich Docks from an early age. He worked in agriculture for some years, then joined the Probation Service in 1967. Since 1995 he has pursued a career as a marine artist specialising in traditional craft - particularly barges! He is a member of the East Anglian Group of Marine Artists and is a keen east coast sailor in his Fisher 31, *MERRIELANDS*, having owned a boat of some sort since the age of seventeen. Married with two grown up daughters he lives near Diss in Norfolk.

Angus Stirling, the illustrator of these pages, was born in Scotland and studied drawing, painting and lithography in Glasgow from 1953 to 1959. After serving with the Royal Air Force he worked for some years in London as a graphic designer, later founding his own design studio. He left the commercial world and moved to Suffolk in 1985, concentrating on fine art, teaching and writing. A one-time member of the East Anglian Group of Marine Artists, he now lives and works in New Zealand.

Thanks are due to Gerald Smy (Harold's son), Brian Pinner, Richard Walsh, and Phillippa Kennedy for typing the original manuscript. The assistance of Barry Pearce in reading the typescript and preparing the schedule of vessels is gratefully acknowledged by the author and publisher, as is his provision of the photograph of the *BEATRICE MAUD* which appears on the back cover.

In 1995 I was visiting an old friend, Jim Ackroyd, who had suffered a stroke and was recovering in Ipswich Hospital. Jim had spent a lot of time speaking to David Poole, who at that time was resident artist at the hospital.

David had got to know Harold Smy and had done some superb paintings and drawings of him. He also planned to write and illustrate a small book about Harold but was looking for a 'collaborator' to interview Harold and get a text together. Jim, knowing of my interest in the world of Thames sailing barges, suggested my name and thus the 'collaboration' began!

Over the next few months I came to know Harold well. By then he was 93 years old but he remembered his eventful life with a great deal of clarity. Interviewing him could be a painful business! Harold was a tactile man and rather deaf so I had to sit very close to him. When he wanted to emphasise something he would back up his statement with a slap on my leg or, if he thought I had got something wrong, a thump on my arm!

Then disaster. David Poole tragically died in December 1995. However, I decided to continue to see Harold and, in any case, by then he had become a good old pal. In 1996 Angus Stirling, a very versatile artist, volunteered to produce a folio of drawings so that the project could continue. And then Harold died after a very short illness.

To some extent, the project to produce a book died too, and my life moved into other very busy directions. However, it has always been in the back of my mind to complete the book and 2004 saw renewed enthusiasm.

It must be emphasised that this story is largely as told to me by Harold. There may well be historical details that are inaccurate or exaggerated. A few of his amusing anecdotes have seen the light of day elsewhere, attributed to others in his trade. Nevertheless there is much in these words which adds to our understanding of the sailing barge trades, told in a way that says a lot about the resilience of this grand old-timer from the days of sail, and the lives of the sailormen working the familiar tan sailed barges up and down the East Coast of England and across to France and Belgium. Those were days that we now tend to romanticise but which were in reality, tough, anxiety ridden and sometimes poverty-stricken.

Despite the hardships, Harold enjoyed his life immensely and it was a privilege for me to share some of it with him in his latter days.

Anthony Osler
Norfolk
2006

For David Poole, who involved me in the project,
and to all Sailormen, past and present.

Chapter 1

EARLY DAYS

"Well, mate, that's a very different place now to what that was when I was a boy - that certainly is!" This is Harold Smy, whose life and times are chronicled in this book, speaking of his birthplace, Pin Mill, on the banks of the River Orwell in Suffolk.

Boyhood at Pin Mill

To romantic yachtsmen and women, the very name Pin Mill conjures up thoughts of picking up a mooring or dropping anchor after a blustery sail from the Deben, the Ore, or the Blackwater and negotiating the muddy hard towards the ever-welcoming lights of the Butt & Oyster – the best waterside pub for many a mile. Pin Mill has been called the Mecca of East Coast yachtsmen and that every one of them will drop anchor there at least once during their yachting career. The sad fact is that many yachts now sail straight past Pin Mill to the comfort and convenience of marinas at Woolverstone and Ipswich, but there are still hundreds of yacht moorings stretching a mile either side of the extensive hard occupied by those who prefer the solitude and tradition of a mooring.

"No, mate, when I was a boy you hardly ever saw a yacht but there was always somethin' goin' on. Barges loading and unloading - barges being repaired. No-one was unemployed - you either worked on the farms or on the barges if you lived at Pin Mill - but more likely on the barges."

Harold Jack Smy was born on 21st November 1902, the fourth of eight children in a cottage 'up the lane' - a little group of houses set back from the boatyards and waterfront cottages and inaccessible during the top of high spring tides. Harold is a bit uncertain, but thinks he was born in Rose Cottage, now occupied by cartoonist Keith Waite and his wife, Rene, - author of several little boaty books.

Growing up

Harold's father, William, was a Pin Mill man, born in 1858. His mother, Bertha, came from the nearby port of Harwich - ideal parents for a man who spent nearly 77 years earning a living from the water. Father was skipper of the *DRACHENFELS* of Harwich, a small spritsail barge of 29 Registered Tons built by the Rhine in 1845. She was one of several craft owned by John Pattrick's cement works at Dovercourt, that mainly carried septaria (cement stone) from the imported stone heaps off Shotley to the factory quay at Phoenix Dock.

Harold had three bothers; Fred (older than Harold), Frank, and George. Fred worked on barges for most of his life – mainly with the London and Rochester Trading Company. He became known to the barging fraternity as 'Uzzers' from his antics of trying to get loaded or unloaded before other barges on turn, convincing wharf foremen and shipworkers "Us is first". Frank was a docker in Ipswich for most of his working life but 'dabbled' in barges every now and then, most notably when he steered *PHOENICIAN* from Pin Mill to Sittingbourne in Kent when she was towed there by *BEATRICE MAUD* skippered by Harold. Brother George did

Father

a small amount of barging when he was a young man, against his mother's wishes, but soon became a career soldier, ending his working life as owner of the Cliff Café in Felixstowe. It is said that Harold's mother, Bertha, was determined to keep one of her sons away from the water and she eventually succeeded with George!

Of his four sisters Hilda and Muriel were older and Doris and Beattie were younger. Doris married Charlie Webb of the famous Pin Mill family; Muriel became a Salvationist and married late in life; poor Beattie died young, shortly after marrying the owner of a Norwich fish and chip shop.

"I went to school at Chelmo." (Chelmondiston, on the Ipswich to Shotley road) says Harold, but my eldest brother, Fred, and two of my sisters went to Woolverstone - blowed if I know why. There was never a school at Pin Mill. I used to spend school holidays afloat with my father. I remember two of the barges he had at the time - *THE SISTERS* and the *THREE SISTERS* - both owned by Ipswich Malting Company."

By the time Harold was in his teens he was well versed in the ways of a boat and the idiosyncrasies of tide and wind. He was rapidly acquiring that instinct which told him to use the elements to one's advantage and not to needlessly fight against them. So when he left school at the age of 13 - eighteen months after the start of the First World War - he was a useful asset to any barge skipper. That skipper was 'Sidie' Read from Manningtree who was in charge of the sailing barge *WINIFRED*, owned by the London and Rochester Barge Company.

Mother

"I was earning ten shillings a week - about four shillings more than I would have got on a bloody farm and more money that I'd ever had in my life. At that time we were loading pitch at Halifax works in Ipswich and shippin' it to Calais - they used it to build roads I

think. Sometimes we'd sail from Calais to London and bring somethin' or another back from London."

"We were unloadin' in Calais one day and the skipper and mate went ashore for a drink. I was left in charge of the cookin'. Something or another distracted my attention and I wasn't keeping an eye on things. The plumb duff boiled dry and exploded, making a hell of a bloody mess everywhere! Old Sidie wasn't none too pleased and I was a bit upset about it too! By the way, they called me Toby in those days – blowed if I can tell you why."

"Old Sidie – he was a rum ole boy – I can tell you. He used to be a semi professional boxer and wasn't afraid to use his fists. On one occasion, when another barge, which should have given way, collided with him and sort of ranged up alongside o' him, Sidie leapt onto the barge, clouted the skipper on the nose and got back onto his own barge just before they separated! Dear, oh dear … he was a lad, that Sidie."

Harold stayed in the *WINIFRED* for just over two years, rapidly growing into a fully-fledged bargeman and setting the scene for his long and eventful working life.

"I was coming over Stoke Bridge (in Ipswich) one day and bumped into my brother Fred. He was mate of the *ALAN* - another L.R.B.C. barge. His skipper Charlie Brown from Rochester urgently needed a third hand - would I like the job? I'd heard that Charlie was a good skipper and I

Spoiling the plum duff

was ready for a change so I said cheerio to the *WINIFRED* and signed up on board the *ALAN*. The work wasn't that much different - cotton seed and linseed from London to Ipswich and pitch from Ipswich to Calais, St. Valery, Dunkirk, Treport and Dieppe. We used to whitewash the hold of the barge to stop the pitch sticking to it. That pitch was rum old stuff, I can tell you!

"One day we were trying to get into Boulogne sur Mer - (of course there were no engines aboard barges in those days - it was sail or nothing) when the bloody leech rope broke and the mainsail came half down. We couldn't get into Boulogne so we

bore away for Dieppe. At dusk we anchored off Calais and the skipper and mate went down below. I was told off to look out for planes - the war was still on. It was pitch dark and I was freezin' half to death when I heard this roarin' sound. Christ, I thought,

Porpoises pretending to be German warplanes

it's a bloody plane! I shouted at the skipper down the bloody hatch. He was shoutin' and swearin', trying to find his money in case we were sunk and cracked 'is 'ead comin' up on deck. He wasn't very happy, I can tell you. The roarin' got louder and louder but it sounded different to a plane noise. 'Ventually, we made out what it was - a bloody great shoal of porpoises goin' by - I've never heard nothin' like it - not before nor since!"

When daylight came, the disabled *ALAN* got under way again, in an attempt to make Dieppe. Harold was 'told off' to do the crew's washing which he hung out on a line on the davits, but as the barge entered Dieppe it hit the pier and snapped the 'linen line'. Most of the washing finished up in Dieppe harbour.

There goes the washing

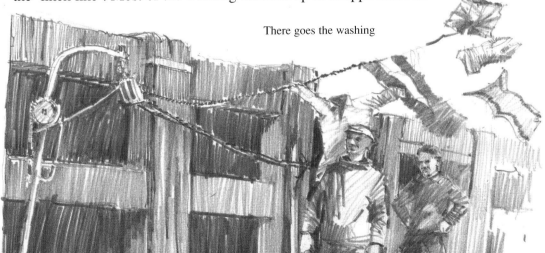

"Some trips are like that," says Harold, "every bloody thing goes wrong. Another time it's all plain sailing. You just can't say. Anyway, we tried to get the French to repair our mainsail but they either couldn't or wouldn't, so me and my brother did the best we could with it. Then we tried to get unloaded at Dieppe but they wouldn't have it. No, you're s'posed to be in Boulogne so that's where you'll have to go. So all the way back to bloody Boulogne. Blimey, mate, that was a trip and a half, that one was!"

Until now Harold's sailing had been confined to the Thames Estuary, the Thames itself and some French Channel ports, but now the chance came for a trip 'down Channel' - with all the attendant excitement conjured up by those two words.

"My first trip down Channel was on board the *ALAN* - towards the end of the war. We got orders to take 150 tons of coal from Goole to Gweek in Cornwall. The freight was £6 a ton and that was a hell of a lot of money in those days, at least ten times what we would have got in peace time. The owners of the barge took half that and we had the other half. Mind you - that took weeks, that trip - I can't remember exactly how long."

A new suit of sails

Chapter 2

TO BE A SAILORMAN

To those of us living in the technological age of the 21st century, life aboard a sailing barge sounds like a wonderful way to make a living. It is true that bargemen did a little better than those who worked on farms but, for many, the security of a weekly pay packet was not there. A few firms paid their crew a weekly wage - R. & W. Paul of Ipswich was one of them - but most operated on the share system. Freightage, i.e. the amount paid by the merchant to move goods from A to B, was traditionally divided into two - half to the owners, who were responsible for maintenance, insurance and replacement of their fleet, and half to the skipper who had to pay his crew, buy the food and fuel for cooking and heating, and pay harbour dues. The skipper would also have to pay for a tug if one were needed and for the use of a 'huffler', an additional hand with local knowledge taken on to work a barge up a tortuous creek or under bridges. Later on, when auxiliary engines were installed in some barges, the skipper also had to pay for his diesel fuel.

The problem with the share system was that no one got paid until the cargo was delivered and there were times when a barge could be wind-bound in some out of the way creek for days - even weeks. At times this made life very difficult indeed for the crews of barges and their families but, at other times a fast round trip with a full hold in both directions could be infinitely more profitable that a weekly wage. Towards the end of the First World War, with a great deal of merchant shipping sunk by the Germans, freight rates were very high. Prudent skippers made enough to buy their houses outright and put money aside for harder times.

Some people say that bargemen earned a little more than farm workers because of the fear factor. There isn't much to be afraid of on a farm - except an unpredictable bull, perhaps! - but aboard a barge, particularly in winter, there can be continual anxiety, especially regarding the weather. There were no radios and no weather forecasts. A barge skipper - responsible for his crew and his cargo - stood alone, dependent on his experience and his common sense. These were the days when men with little or no education, but good, solid and true, could be given awesome responsibility, with the lives and livelihood of others solely in their hands. Another example of this was engine driving in the days of steam, a difficult craft learned over many years. Take the superb Mallard which, in 1938, set the world speed record for a steam locomotive at 126 m.p.h.. It is quite sobering to think that after the go-ahead to try for the record was given by Mallard's designer, Sir Nigel Gresley, the final decision was taken by driver Duddington who, ably assisted by fireman T. Bray, had to apply every ounce of his hard-earned skill to achieve that feat, which remains unbeaten to the present day.

Gear failures were common, especially in strong winter winds. Taking a barge the forty miles between Southend and Tower Bridge could be particularly hazardous, especially at night. There were countless collisions and accidents on the Thames, which was a much more heavily congested river than it is today, with thousands of sailing craft, lighters, steamers and tugs jostling for position, each with their own understanding of the collision regulations!

A barge requires bursts of energy to keep it going and crews needed to be in good physical condition. Getting in 30 fathoms (180 feet, 55 metres) of anchor chain against a force six wind and a sluicing ebb tide, can be extremely arduous work. Likewise, brailing up a mainsail requires a fast input of energy that many a land-based worker would not be able to do. 'Chubb' Horlock, a barge skipper from Mistley and a great friend of Harold said 'A barge'll keep you fit, if not rich.'

Chubb Horlock

Bargemen were always worrying about getting home. Being stuck miles from a railway station or bus route often meant weekends away from home and family. But would many of them have changed places with workers on shore? Some, yes. Some did, undoubtedly. But most had enough salt water in their veins and Stockholm tar on their hands to love the life sufficiently to endure its privations.

The barge blocks at Pin Mill

Chapter 3

HAROLD GETS PROMOTION

During the 1914-1918 war, the fortunes of the Smy family improved significantly. They moved from Pin Mill to Whip Street, Ipswich, eliminating the nine mile walk home when the barge finished up at Ipswich. Harold's father became part-owner of the barge *LANDFIELD*, in partnership with Mr. Bill Rogers of the Ipswich Malting Company. The barge cost the men £600 to buy. This project must have prospered, for a year or two later, Mr. Smy Senior purchased two houses in Suffolk Road, Ipswich, letting one of them to a barber from the old Ipswich firm Wootons. When Harold was 16 in 1919, he said goodbye to the *ALAN* and joined his part barge-owner father aboard the *LANDFIELD*.

"Christ, mate, he was bloody strict" remembers Harold, "and because my father was part-owner, we had to do maintenance work as well. We once went aboard a big old sailing ship with a hold full of timber from Norway or Sweden or somewhere, and did a deal with them for enough wood to repair the ceiling - the lining or floor at the bottom of the hold on the barge - which had been badly damaged by grabs and shovels. It only cost us a fiver plus the cost of all the drills I broke doing the work!"

"The *LANDFIELD* was in the ballast trade a lot of the time; sand, shingle, that sort of thing. Shingle came off the beach and the exposed knolls at Felixstowe Ferry at the entrance to the river Deben. Loading was hard work, shovelling the shingle into wheel-barrows and pushing them up a springy old plank on to the barge which was deliberately run aground to make loading easier. We nosed our way into all sorts of places with ballast, like Wilford Bridge beyond Woodbridge, and Snape Maltings. Both these trips needed hufflers to get up them narrow little channels. It's amazing where a barge would go. You could sometimes see masts and sails miles inland and think to yourself 'how the hell did they get there?' Mind you, a barge'll do anything except speak, if there's a little bit of wind!"

"Ipswich Malting Company owned a barge called *MARY ANN* and the skipper was a bloke called Hooker. He always had leaf in his mouth! Some old boys used to suck on a match stalk, but not Hooker - he preferred leaves; hell if I can tell you why. Anyway, it was the time when we were mending the hold of the *LANDFIELD* and old Hooker called my father ashore. I couldn't hear what they were a sayin' but eventually my father came back on board the *LANDFIELD* and he say 'Mr. Hooker wants you to do a job for him. He's got to go into hospital to have something done to his teeth and he want the *MARY ANN* takin' down to Shotley to load barley. He's cleared it with Mr. Damant (the Chairman of Ipswich Malting Company) – who apparently said 'He's only a boy!' to which Mr. Hooker had replied 'Well, if he's a boy, he does a man's job!'"

"That was my first taste as skipper at the age of 17. I took MARY ANN down to Shotley and took barley off a ship anchored in the eddy (approximately where the entrance to Shotley marina runs into deep water today) and brought it back to Ipswich. The regular mate came with me. I recollect I got 50 shillings for that little trip!

"When I was still 17, I became skipper of the CRYALLS owned by my father and Mr. Rogers - same as the LANDFIELD. She carried only 80 tons and was in poor condition. Trouble was I couldn't earn enough in her - remember we were only paid freightage, but I stuck it for two or three years and left to go mate in the RAVEN around 1922."

"RAVEN was built by the London and Rochester Barge Company Limited, of Rochester, and hired from them and named by Marriages of Colchester, the flour millers. Another of their barges, EAST ANGLIA was under the same arrangement."

"Skipper of the RAVEN was a bloke called Bill French; a good skipper, but a crafty old customer. He lived in Colchester and he always managed somehow to finish up there, leavin' me to get back to Ipswich! In the end I decided I'd had enough of

Colchester and came back to Ipswich Dock where there was always a job goin' of some sort or another - it was a very busy place in them days. I could have taken the CRYALLS again but she was getting very ancient and as I said, she wasn't really big enough to earn a livin' in. So I got a job with R. & W. Paul aboard their lighter called the P.1. I was paid a flat wage of £3 a week."

Marriages hired the RAVEN from the L.R.B.C.

"The P.1. had no power of its own. It was always towed by a tug or, more often, behind one of Paul's steamers, FIRECREST more often than not. It was built in

Wivenhoe on the Colne and carried 500 tons of grain. She was 138 feet long and built of steel and had a proper cabin and all that. We often went to Antwerp and loaded wheat for King's Lynn or Ipswich. The skipper of the *P.1.* was Nipper Gray, who lived in King's Lynn, so obviously he preferred to finish up there. Still, never mind, we always got a train ticket home, so that was somethin'. I arrived home in Ipswich once and a bloke from Pauls came to the house and said 'Burroughs (a stand-by mate) won't go to Belgium, so you'll have to go back to Lynn'. He gave me a rail ticket and that was the end of my break! On dear yes, they did what they bloody well liked with yer then. No-one would stand for it now!"

" 'Ventually, the *P.1.* was sold to a firm on the Humber and was used in the coal trade, but it got sunk and Pauls bought it back agin. When the lighter wasn't working, I used to be sent down to the shipyard to do maintenance work. The yard, called St. Clement's Shipyard at Dock End, Ipswich, was owned by Pauls and used for maintaining their own vessels. They built barges there too, in the early part of the century. *DORIS* was built there in 1904 and so was *GRAVELINES I* in 1905 and *GRAVELINES II* in 1906. Mind you, they were the *HILDA* and the *ENA* then. The French named them *GRAVELINES I* and *II* when they bought them in 1907. Then Pauls brought *GRAVELINES II* back in 1912 and re-named her *BIJOU* - wunnerful ain't it."

The St. Clement's Shipyard at the Dock End, Ipswich

17

"We came out of Antwerp one night aboard the *P.1.*. That was a bit blowy, and Nipper went down below to make some coffee, leaving me to steer. The lighter needed steerin' - 'specially when fully-loaded in a bumpy sea. Some steamer skippers hated towin' the lighter; that gave them somethin' else to have to worry about. Anyway, I was steerin' away and started to feel a little queasy. It wasn't the sea that was doin' it, it was a paraffin lamp in the wheel house. So I put it out. When Nipper came back with the coffee he went mad! 'Sposin' we break the tow, how the hell will we know where we are with the light out!' I thought that was a bloody funny thing for an experienced man like Nipper to say, but there you are."

"The blocks (baulks of timer half sunk into the mud to support a flat bottomed craft for cleaning and maintenance) at St. Clement's yard weren't big enough for the *P.1.* so we had to take her up to London if we wanted to scrub 'er off. Oh dear, she was a rum ol' craft was that *P.1.*"

"Still, one day, in 1927 I think, some of us were standin' about near the Custom House (by Ipswich Dock) not doin' a lot I 'spec' 'cept gossipin', when Pauls' man, Bob Peck, shouted at me to go down the shipyard. 'Parently the mizzen aboard the *GIPPING* needed repairing. So off I went and did the work and Mr. Peck, he say, 'Where's your mate?' I said, 'I didn't know I was skipper!' Anyway, that's how I got the *GIPPING*. She was built at Dock End Shipyard in 1889 and was used mainly between Ipswich and London. She nearly always took grain of some sort or another, but sometimes sugar."

"There was always a bit of jealousy around whenever someone got promoted or got a better barge. Sid Garnham from Shotley thought he should ha' got the *GIPPING*. 'Ventually he got the tiller steered *EMILY* so that quietened him down a bit. In the end Sid gave up barging to work at

All kinds of craft in the London River.

Barges, tugs, lighters

the Picture House cinema in Ipswich town, but he fell off a gantry and died. Poor ol' Sid."

" 'Cos in them days the Thames was packed solid with ships of all kinds - barges, tugs, lighters, steamers, square-riggers and pilot boats. There were plenty of collisions and near misses and plenty of swearin' - everyone jostling for position. When we was in one of the docks or alongside a big old square-rigger, stevedores did the loadin' and we did the trimmin'. Corn was in sacks and if that weren't properly trimmed it could shift when you were underway - 'specially in a bit of a blow - and then you could be in real trouble. Yes, mate, we always did our own trimmin'. Maize was in 18 stone sacks, and barley and oats in 12 stone sacks. You were ready for a pint after trimmin' a hundred and twenty tons o' them, I can tell you! You had to be careful not to let any maize get into the bilges - that could stink the bloody place out when it went rotten! Some of the sacks had holes in 'em and we used to break these open and use the maize to fill in the gaps between the sacks so's to pack as much in the hold as possible."

"I remember when we were unloading maize on Ipswich Dock one day and old Billy Paul - one of the guv'nors - came along in his hard hat and made someone sweep maize out of the railway lines! Mind you, that's 'ow they made their bloody money."

"Talking about Ipswich Dock, when I was about 26 or 27, I knew a bloke called Frank Goddard. He was mate of the *WAVENEY* - a little old Paul's barge that loaded about 110 tons. We were sitting in the Wherry pub playing dominoes when there was a hell of a rumpus outside. Apparently, a bullock on its way to

The bullock in the Dock

Ipswich market had cut away from 'is mates, run amok and finished up falling into the dock. Frank and me jumped into a barge boat, chased after the bullock which was swimmin' around, got a rope around his head and towed him down to the lock gates where there's a little beach. The old bullock found his feet and off he went agin - towards the gasworks. There was a slaughterhouse in Fore Street in them days so the old bullock didn't have far to go!

"Mr. Mercer, the butcher in Fore Street, said you'll get a reward for this. Goddard wanted his money there and then, so I gave him five shillings to keep him quiet. I went off to the Evening Star in Carr Street and told them the story and they paid me £2.10s.0d. (£2.50) for it, so I gave Goddard another pound."

"Frank finished up as mate in the steel *SPERANZA*, a Goldsmith's barge. He went ashore at Woolwich one night, came back three-quarters drunk, strangled the skipper who was asleep in his bunk and went off with the skipper's money! The barge lay there with no riding light and apparently no-one on board, so the police went to have a look round. They found the skipper dead."

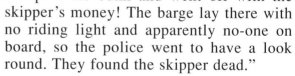

"Frank Goddard was 'ventually caught. He was hung in London. Yes, he was a nasty piece of furniture, was Frank - always hungry for money. Dear, oh dear!"

Stumpies

Chapter 4

ABOARD THE TIME MACHINE

A study of painting and photography depicting the maritime scenes of the first four decades of the 20th century will reveal a very different picture to that which exists today. Two painters in particular, W. L. Wyllie and Charles Dixon, had the superb knack of showing the activity and congestion of the Thames in all its glory. Those days will never be seen again. A voyage today from Ipswich to the Lower Pool in London - a trip undertaken by Harold on countless occasions - would be a relatively barren experience, with a few container ships, a pilot cutter perhaps, the occasional tug, a yacht or power boat or two and the dead or dying remains of the once busiest waterway in the world for a backdrop. For Harold and his generation it was a completely different story. Let us step back in time for a trip from Ipswich to London with Harold.

"You should have seen Ipswich Dock in those days, mate! Packed solid sometimes. Twenty or thirty barges belonging to Pauls or Cranfields - often lightering grain from big square-riggers anchored down river. There would have been some smaller square-riggers in the dock unloadin' timber from Scandinavia. There were some rum old boys on some of them - you stayed well clear of 'em when they'd had a few drinks!"

Cranfield's Mill on Ipswich Dock

" 'Cos there was a big gasworks on the dockside, so there was a continuous procession of small coasting steamers from up North. Yes, mate, there was always something goin' on. And o' course there was a railway running all round the dock, linked up to the mainline near Ipswich station."

"Anyway, mate, we're off to London on our imaginary voyage with 120 tons of malting barley for Charrington's. We'll lock out on the half ebb so's we'll get to Harwich just nicely to catch seven hours of flood to get us into the Thames with a bit o' luck. You've got to work yer tides on this job, mate. There's a touch of North in the wind so we should be OK today. We're through the lock now away down the River Orwell. No power station (now gone) or Orwell Bridge then, but plenty of industry over to starboard."

"We're soon through Woolverstone and can see the Cat House where they were supposed to put a cut-out of a cat in the window if the preventive men (customs) were about, to warn the smugglers to stay clear. Whether that's true or not, I couldn't tell yer!"

"And then down to Pin Mill, where I was born. There's quite a lot going on - barges being loaded and unloaded on the hard and, o' course, barges and other wooden vessels being repaired. Quite a few people worked at Pin Mill - hard work an' all - so the old Butt and Oyster did well! Now we're down to Butterman's Bay and we're in luck. No less than three hefty old square-riggers, too big and too deep in their draught to get up to Ipswich. Look at them barges! They're clusterin' around like piglets at an old sow. They want to get loaded up

The Butt & Oyster, Pin Mill

by the time the tide turns so they can get back to Ipswich in time for tea! I know, mate, 'cos I've done plenty on it."

"Wunnerful aint it? Them old square-riggers have probably been towed all the way from Dover by tug. There's no way they'd risk sailin' through the sandbanks of the Thames estuary."

"Harwich, here we come! Always somethin' happening in the harbour, particularly as it's an important naval base still using steam power. So just look at that! Coaling

23

ships, water boats, jolly boats, and everything else connected to the Navy. There's ferries plying between Harwich, Felixstowe, and Shotley. There's a small dock at Felixstowe - a basic cut into the sea wall - nothing like it is now mate with all them container ships. See those smacks over there? They're shrimpers and they're boiling their catch on the way home for all them day trippers at Harwich and Dovercourt."

Harwich Harbour

"It's low water now but there's enough water to cross the Stone Banks over to the Naze and we'll pick up a lovely flood to take us up the Wallet. No, no, mate! Going to London is up the Wallet. Down the Wallet is comin' home. Don't let me hear you say different."

"I reckon I can see twenty or thirty barges today, many of them on their way into Harwich to catch a tide to Pin Mill, Ipswich, or up the Stour to Mistley. And way ahead of us, although we'll overtake 'em in the Swin, are a couple of stackies; hay and straw up to London for the horses and muck back for the farms. We'll give 'em a shout when we catch 'em up. Barges used as stackies have to have their rigging adjusted so that the straw can be stacked half-way up the mast. 'Cos you can't see where you're goin' half the time, so someone sits on the stack keepin' a lookout and giving directions to whoever's on the wheel. Tha's a rum old job in the London River, mate, I can tell you."

"All London-bound vessels are heading for the Spitway, a shallow gap in the sands between

Seeing what they can get

For Maldon with timber

the southerly end of the Wallet and the Swin. Now, if we'd approached this at dead low water we'd have had to wait around until the flood had made an hour or more before there was enough water. But we're alright today. Just look over there to starboard! Several barges bound for Colchester or Maldon and a few smacks seeing what they can get. In the winter there'll be hundreds of 'em, from Tollesbury, Mersea and Brightlingsea. In the summer many of the smacksmen are away on the big yachts - you know, mate - the J-class yachts and the like."

"It's more or less due south to the Whitaker buoy and then we skirt around the end of the Foulness and Maplin Sands into the London river proper. We're pickin' up some traffic from up north now - small tramp steamers and boomie barges bringing coal and taking the slightly shorter route through the Swin or the Barrow Deep. Look over there to port and you can see some of the 'big boys' in the Black Deep, hull down. Much deeper water out there."

25

"Now here's the first of our stackies! Take the wheel mate, and I'll give 'em a shout. 'Whe're yer for?' I think 'e said Barking Creek, but I couldn't be sure."

"Over to starboard, on the Maplin Sands, the Leigh cockle boats are just comin' afloat. They dry out on the ebb, rake the shellfish up, and then wait for the flood to lift 'em off and take 'em back home - wunnerful ain't it? Our aim is to get into the Lower Hope, just past Canvey, before the tide turns. The tide runs like a bloody train on the Thames, mate. So we'll anchor in the Lower Hope, have a bit of a bite, and sit tight 'til the morning. If we were really desperate, which we're not, we'd be underway again in six hours time when the ebb will have done its worst, but we don't want to be sailing at night, not today. No, no, that's not a lot of fun in a barge at night with big old steamers chargin' about."

Taking the cockles back home

"We shan't be alone in the Lower Hope. Tha's a favourite anchorage for all manner of craft. An' we can sit on deck watchin' all the stuff comin' down on the ebb. I hope you like rabbit mate, 'cos that's what we've got tonight. My old mate Charlie brought 'em up to my house last night. I didn't ask him where he'd got 'em from!"

"Come on here! Shake your bloody self and get that stove stoked up. I can't sail up to London without bacon and eggs in me belly. Another nice day with a useful breeze and the ebb has nearly gone so we'll get underway as soon as we've had breakfast. Now we've got to be sharp and keep our eyes open, 'specially when we get near Gravesend. See what's comin' up astern - a big old square-rigger bein' towed by a tug - probably from The Downs, like the ones in the Orwell. Smaller sailing ships are much more manoeuvrable, 'specially those with fore and aft sail, and they can delay taking an expensive tug until much farther up the river. Do I ever take a tug? Not if I can bloody well help it mate, 'cept Yarmouth in certain conditions of wind and tide. Yarmouth can be tricky."

"It's getting busy now what with customs boats, health boats, pilot boats, water boats, coaling ships, tugs towin' lighters, barges and steamers. And getting' dirty too, what with all the soot and smoke and grime. There's some big old mooring buoys hereabouts which we need to look out for; the tide can carry you down on 'em so easy. You'd know about it if you 'it one! Too bloody right mate."

"Well we've got through Gravesend reach without 'ittin' anything and now we've got to contend with Tilbury. See over there mate, two old ships from Nelson's day; the *WORCESTER* and the *ARETHUSA* - both now used as training ships for the Merchant Navy. Thank Christ I didn't finish up on one of them!"

Close hauled in the London River

Wapping

"The old ferry's busy today. I think half the population of Tilbury work in Gravesend and vice versa. And we'll have to keep an eye open for stuff comin' out of Tilbury Docks. In this nor' westerly we'll have to make a couple of tacks; wind'll be on our nose for a mile or so, but the flood tide will be running full up Northfleet Hope - then a nice clear run to Erith Reach. Keep yer eyes skinned mate; you can never trust all these other boats to keep to the rules of the road!"

"It starts to get really busy now. Just past Barking Creek on the starboard side we come to the eastern entrance to the Royal Docks where they can take really big ships. There's not a lot of room for manoeuvre when one o' them is bein' tugged in or out. And around here there's another hazard - small lighters with only the tide to drive 'em. Each one has a licensed waterman on board with a large oar the lightermen call paddles, to help steer, but otherwise she's at the mercy of the wind and tide. Tha's a very skilled job, mate, and the watermen earn a pile of money, but give me an old barge any day."

"We're on our way to a little dock just beyond Cherry Garden pier on the port side and a bit below Tower Bridge. But we'll have to jump about a bit before we get there. It's a beat up Bugsby's Reach and another one up Limehouse Reach, where the river starts getting' a bit narrow, plus dealing with the western locks of the Royal Docks, the four entrances to the Millwall Docks on

28

the Isle of Dogs and, on our port side, goin' up the river, the entrances to the Rotherhithe Docks. These docks employ thousands and thousands of men, some of 'em on day work, so the poor sods have to turn up everyday not knowin' if there's work for 'em or not. A lot of smaller ships, like us for instance, don't always have to go into the docks to load or unload or both, 'cos the river up here is lined with warehouses that have their own dock or quay. Mind you, at low water your barge dries out aground, but that don't matter mate, tha's what they were made to do!"

"Mind you, we often do go into one or other of the docks, and that can be a rum ole job without an engine. You can sometimes set a topsail and sail across a dock but, sooner or later, you have to warp her alongside other lighters and barges and you can get bashed about somethin' cruel. Sometimes you get some help and a free tow but mostly you have to fend for yourself and give as good as you get. You know what I mean, mate!"

"Well, here we are mate, another little trip and no damage done. There's another barge on our spot, waiting for high water to get away, so we'll just slip alongside o' him and then sort the ropes out when he wants to be away. He's one of my good old pals, anyway, so with a bit o' luck he'll be brewing up a cuppa. What do think about that view, mate? Tower Bridge, St Pauls, the Tower and all that. I always get a little thrill when we come round the bend and see that lot!"

St. Pauls lofty dome towers over the busy Thames

A small 'stack' of timber

30

Chapter 5

A WIFE AND TWO NEAR MISSES!

"If ever I was in London at the weekend, I'd get to a football match. Well, one Saturd'y I'd gone to see Fulham play. This is 1923 we're talking about now. I can't remember who they were playing or whether they won or lost but that don't matter. After the match I went down to Hammersmith Market to buy some thread and some woman said 'You come from Norfolk don't you?' and I said 'No, no, no; I come from Suffolk! Not bloody Norfolk.' Then she pointed to her friend and said 'She comes from Suffolk, too.' So I get chattin' to this Suffolk gal and she tells me her name is Alice Kemp and that she comes from Bungay - so I called her 'Bung'! She was working for two old ladies who lived up there in London but later they moved to Burlington Road in Ipswich, so that was a lot better."

"Anyway, we got married in 1926 at St. Margaret's Church in Ipswich and I'll tell you what old mate, I couldn't ha' done better if I'd looked around for another fifty years! We had three children; Gerald, born in 1928, Donald in 1932 and Kathleen in 1936. Gerald came with me on the barge towards the end of the war right through to 1957."

"When we married we lived with my mother and father at 36 Suffolk Road. Then we rented 23 Christchurch Street. Bung used to do weekly washing for a Mr. Sherwood who finally went to live with his daughter in Bournemouth. He asked 'Is there anything you want out of the house?' I chose a coal scuttle and Bung had some sheets and pillowcases and a wardrobe. Bung used to go fruit pickin' - not for herself mind, but to make a bit o' money to give to the pensioners for a day trip to Yarmouth. She was a good woman like that, was Bung; she'd do anything to help anyone. And she loved animals - that she did."

"In 1938 we moved to 2 Union Street for a short while, then 124 Cemetery Road where I've lived ever since. In September 1940, a German parachute bomb fell on Cemetery Road and they wouldn't let anyone near. Bugger that, I thought and I went through other people's gardens and all over the bloody place 'til I was home. Luckily we hadn't been damaged, but the bomb had only partly exploded and a couple of days later we had to leave the house whilst they detonated it. About 70 houses were totally destroyed and hundreds damaged. We just lost a few panes of glass."

" 'Cos, when you think about it, a barge skipper had to have a bloody good wife, bein' away most of the time and all that. Mind you, there were one or two times when she was totally unsympathetic, like when my boy Gerry's twins were born just before Christmas 1952. Dear, oh dear. I heard the news from the landlord of the Masons Arms, George Elwood, and o'course I had to bloody well celebrate didn't I mate! Dear, oh dear, first of all I tried to get in the wrong bloody house where they weren't too bloody pleased and then when I did 'ventually get home, I shit myself crawlin' up the stairs. 'Bung, Bung.' I called, but her reply weren't too friendly, I can tell you. I can't remember where I slept that night!"

"Bung became ill in 1973 and died in '74. That's one of the reasons I came out of the *BEATRICE MAUD*, apart from the fact that she was fallin' to bits and the Guv'nor wouldn't do nothin' about it. Yes, I wanted to be around her for her last days - she was a good wife and a good mother."

"Well, I stayed in the old *GIPPING* 'til about 1932 or thereabouts and then took the *ELDRED WATKINS*. She belonged to Albert Watkins who had a lime and cement business at Blackwall on the Thames. He had a kiln and all that, and the barge was named after his father."

"Anyway, we were working away lightering grain from a ship in Butterman's Bay on the

Smaller ships worked into the dock

Orwell, 'n takin' it up Ipswich Dock. We'd just left the grain ship when I saw a steamer comin' straight towards us - about a four and a half thousand tonner - and blow me down, it just kept a comin' and cut me down and sunk me. The ship was called *SHEAF GARTH* and had a pilot on board. Anyhows, he turns her around and was he pleased to see me and my mate scrabblin' about in the barge boat!"

"I helped get her up and float her the next day and we beached her at Pin Mill. There was an old boy there who used to break 'em up when they weren't fit for nothin' and he had practically got the stern right off her when old Fred Horlock from Mistley reckoned he could repair her. So Fred bought her; got her back in working order, and renamed her *REVIVAL*! Wunnerful, ain't it?"

"I was walking about a little while after losing the old *ELDRED WATKINS* - you know what I mean, mate - but not for long! I've never been afraid of work and that weren't long before someone came a lookin' for me."

"Paul's needed a skipper for the *BIJOU* (ex. *GRAVELINES II*, ex. *ENA*) and I jumped at the chance. The work was almost entirely in the grain and cattle feed trade and went off without incident right up to the beginning of the war. Just after the war had started, I went up to the Millwall Docks to load maize for Mistley. When I got to Mistley, Frank Ainger shouted at me 'No barges today!' A Gerry bomb had destroyed the quay. A few months later the *BIJOU* was again at Mistley, tied up alongside, and one night she was hit by an incendiary bomb and caught fire. I was at home in Ipswich! When I went to Mistley the next morning they'd shoved the barge out into the river, away from the dockside and buildings to burn away in safety. And that's where she still lies, mate, off the Quay at Mistley for all to see at low water!"

The majestic profile of a coasting thoroughbred

Chapter 6

HAROLD AND THE WARTIME YEARS

"Soon arter the loss of the *BIJOU* I was sent to work at the shipyard - St. Clement's shipyard at the end of the Ipswich dock - just outside the lock gates. Pauls owned the yard then and used it to repair their own barges. There hadn't been a boat built there for thirty-five years or more. I cant remember 'xactly why, but I got fed up and went to work in the brickyard and later at the sugar beet factory. Then I got a job on the lock gates at Ipswich hoping to get onto the tugs. I noticed the auxiliary barge *BEATRICE MAUD* laying at Ipswich doin' nothin' and 'parently no one on board her. She was owned by Sullys down in Kent. So I got in touch with Mr. Sully who said 'If you can get a mate, she's yours.'"

"I soon sorted myself out a mate. I was bloody glad of the chance to get back on the water, that I was, and I became Master of the *BEATRICE MAUD* at Ipswich on 16th February 1941. There were lots of restrictions by then. You couldn't go nowhere without a bit of paper from someone and you weren't allowed to sail at night. Mind you, the winds and tides didn't know there was a bloody war on and getting into a harbour by dark was sometimes a near impossibility. When I started in the *BEATRICE MAUD* we used to go to Lowestoft and Yarmouth a lot. You weren't allowed to run the motor 'cos of fear of mines. 'Parently the sound and vibration attracted them. We also had to go to Tilbury sometimes to be degauzed, which is de-magnetising. Sometimes you would actually see a mine floating about. I shudder to think what we'd have been like if we'd 'it one of 'em!"

"By now, the Government controlled everything and they needed stuff down in the Bristol Channel. I was told to load up and get down to the South Foreland, between Ramsgate and Dover, where a tug would pick me up and take me into Dover. When I got there they said there's been bombs at Dover so hang about whilst they sort it out. 'Ventually I went back to Broadstairs and anchored off there for the night, 'cos a hell of a tide runs round that old South Foreland!"

Outer harbour, Dover

"Anyway, next morning away we go. By now we're in a convoy with naval ships protectin' us and all that. I'm number 'leven and we have to keep to five knots. All went well 'til we got down to the West country when that starts to kick up a very rough sea with a nasty ole head wind. I'm havin' a hell of a job to keep up! I was number 'leven - now I'm bloody sixteenth! 'Cos the engine on the *BEATRICE MAUD* was only an auxiliary. That weren't built to push me through heavy seas and headwinds."

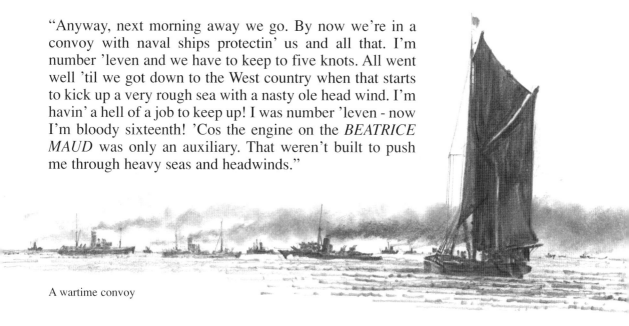

A wartime convoy

"A trawler come up to me and some naval bloke on board shouted across 'Why aren't you keepin' up?' 'It's getting too bad for me', I say, 'I want to go into Plymouth.' The old trawler stand off for a bit and then come back and say 'You've got permission to go to Plymouth' - bloody glad to get rid of me, if you ask me. So off I go and when I git there a Guv'ment boat comes out and tells me to lay in Plymouth sound. Not bloody likely I think - that's too bloody lumpy - so, I ask if I can go to Sutton Quay. 'Oh, you know Sutton Quay do you?' says the bloke. 'Yes mate, I've been there before.' I say (although that was a hell of a long time back), and he lets me go there."

"A corporal in the Army came over - a bloke from Ipswich that I'd once had aboard the *BIJOU* as third hand, Bernie Ward, his name. 'Do you want some fish?' he say. 'Yes, mate.' I replied and gave him five shillun. I've never seen the fish nor yet my five shillun. I'd give him somethin' to be going on with if ever I saw him about, even though that was fifty years ago and more!"

"We lay there for two days when I get orders from the launch to go into the harbour proper - more bloody naval control business. When I git to the main harbour a little old Wren tells me I can go to Falmouth on my own. So off I sets, but the old wind gets up and is blowin' me ashore so I make for Newlyn instead and bugger the bloody Navy. Tha's only a little old harbour but that had black squares on a white sea wall, like a chess board, so's you could see it from quite a distance."

"We ran in to Newlyn and luckily there was a Dutchman loading stone who took a line off us and helped us moor up. Then a bloody corporal jumps aboard with a fixed bayonet. He's shakin' like a bloody leaf! I told him to be quiet 'til I'd tidied up a bit."

An auxiliary sailing barge

"Next mornin' Naval patrol on board agin - I'm getting' used to them now. 'So what are you going to do to me today?' I asked 'em, 'Shoot me, put me in prison, or drown me!' I think they saw the funny side. Anyway, the Naval bloke asked, 'Whe're are you for?' 'Bristol,' I say, 'and I'm only in a wooden box!' He told me that five of the original ships in the convoy that had set out from Dover had been torpedoed by E Boats. Thank Christ I went into Plymouth! 'Wait here for two days,' he says 'and then an Air Force launch will escort you to St. Ives.

"The following day we made Avonmouth and Bristol the next day - up what they call the Gore. There was a hospital nearby where we unloaded, and of 'cos we kept wavin' at the nurses when they looked out of the winders!

"I phoned the Guv'nor, Mr. Sully, to see if I could take the sprit off the barge and remove the topm'st and leeboards. That old Atlantic swell would nearly force the leeboards off. Mr Sully say 'All right, but make certain you bring all the bits back when you 'ventually return.'"

"I rigged up a leg o' mutton sail on the mainmast to steady the barge in a swell and we were ready for Merchant Service! By now we were under the total control of the Guv'ment and we got regular pay. I had a Merchant Navy uniform with gold braid on it! A couple of American soldiers stood to attention and saluted me once! I think they thought I was a bloody Admiral!"

"The wheelhouse on the barge had been reinforced with concrete blocks in case we were 'it, so I installed a seat in there with an 'ole in it and a bucket underneath for you know what! We also had a gunner on board, but he couldn't have 'it an 'aystack at 20 yards. He said he hit a Gerry plane in the Bristol Channel, but I know he bloody well didn't!"

Some were unaffected by the war

"We used to get our orders from a Mr. Lovejoy, manager for Cory Brothers in Bristol, 'cos he got 'is orders from the Guv'ment or the Navy or whatever. Mr. Lovejoy's second in command was a Mr. Ayres - a nasty piece of furniture if ever there was one. Mr. Lovejoy told me to carry on just the same as I did on the London River - using a skipper's judgement and all that. Mr. Ayres tried to tell me when to arrive, when to leave, how to load. I think he'd have told me when to go to the toilet given half the chance! In the end I had to go to see Mr. Lovejoy and complain. Mr. Ayres was told not to interfere with the skipper's business and we didn't hear much more from him. I've never taken a lot of nonsense from anyone - no, Sir!"

"We carried all sorts of cargo in-between all the Bristol Channel ports; butter, cement, coal - you name it, we carried it. Once when we were loading cement for Bridgewater at Cardiff we saw Americans unloading tanks in wooden crates, and they were burning the crates! So we rescued the ones waiting for the fire, loaded them on deck and took them to Bridgewater where we sold them to the local 'huffler' - I can't remember his name but he had size 14 feet! Oh yes, mate, you've got to keep your bloody eyes open on this job."

"Another time we loaded tobacco leaves, and, of course some of them found their way into the skipper's cabin, didn't they? I made what they call a prig - 2lbs of leaves soaked in rum and tied up in a sausage shape in canvas and spunyarn. Six months to cure and then you've got it! Lovely smokin' or chewin' tobacco! Slice a bit off when you want it."

"We saw some rum owd things in the war"

"Wherever we went we found a good pub. I was a bit more than friendly with the landlady of the Bridgewater Arms and used to help her with the barrels 'cos her husband was away in the Army. Turned out later that she was the daughter of the Chief Constable! Oh dear, oh dear!"

"I managed to get home three or four times a year and usually took something special like some ham or butter or somethin'. In 1944 my son Gerry left school and came aboard *BEATRICE MAUD* as 4th hand, paid by the Guv'ment and everything. £4 and sixpence a week he got - good money for a 16 year old in those days. Mind you, he had to give me a bit for his keep. Yes, mate, bring 'em up to pay their way, that's my policy."

"When the war ended in 1945 I thought we would pack up and go home, but we were under Naval Orders for another 8 months. Then at last we were let off the hook. We loaded coal for Mr. Sully at Barry and then went back to Bristol for the sprit, the topm'st, leeboards and sails. The leeboards rested on top of the coal which we'd levelled off so's you could almost play billiards on it. We tied 'em down so if we got thrown about in a heavy swell they wouldn't start crashing about, and the spars were lashed down on deck."

"It was an uneventful trip home. We had a pint every night at some pub or another, except at Cowes where we declined a lift ashore from the Navy as we had a lovely joint of beef in the stove that we had picked up in Weymouth! When I say it was an uneventful trip I'm not quite tellin' you the truth! We had planned to get into the Medway by going into the Swale and under Queen's Bridge. We'd spent the night in Ramsgate and come round the North Foreland. Gerry was steering and we could see Whitstable off to port and another barge up ahead when suddenly crunch, crunch! What the bloody hell was that? We'd come to a halt on the Columbine Shoal at the entrance to the Swale! Somebody must have moved the buoy! Anyway we 'ventually float off and go across to another barge, the *KATHLEEN*, and they tell us we can't go through the Swale to the Medway 'cos of anti-submarine barriers still in position. So we anchor for the night and enter the Medway farther up the estuary at Sheerness. Then up to Chatham to unload our coal and our war is over. Yes, mate!"

Weymouth in the days of sail

Chapter 7

THE PEACETIME YEARS

The war was over and the country was beginning to rediscover normality and make some sense of the six nightmare years that had wrecked Europe and brought misery to millions. There was hope and expectation and a searching for the gateway to the elusive golden age. Harold's world was changing fast. The sailing barge fleet had dwindled to a few hundred and road transport was encroaching upon transport by sea and river. But in a country struggling to find its feet again there was work to be done and a living to be made and Harold did just that, staying in *BEATRICE MAUD* until 1974. Here is Harold's story of those years.

"Well, mate, the old ship had done a lot of work and taken a fair old bit of knockin' about in the Bristol Channel so was due for a complete refit. Mr. Sully had done very nicely thank you during the war, what with the Guv'ment paying for the use of his fleet so there was a bit of money in the kitty!"

"So it was off to Sittingbourne for a few weeks on a flat rate - scraping, painting, helping the shipwrights and generally gettin' in the bloody way, I expect. Mind you, there's nothin' much I can't do aboard a barge. I can splice rope and wire, do good solid woodwork and even service an engine. I've never made a sail from scratch but I've done plenty of repairs. We had a new set made for *BEATRICE MAUD* by Pup Wain. She looked bloody smart by the time we'd finished with her, mate."

"Then it was back to work on the share system, where the harder you work the more you can earn - if the wind and tide will let you. My son Gerry was still with me and we did very well in the cargo trade. 'Cos you had to jump about a bit, mate - you had to look for work and make certain you weren't hanging about. I mean, that weren't no good taking something down to Yarmouth and coming back light, was it? Generally Mr. Sully had fixed us up with a return cargo, but if he hadn't or couldn't then I'd chase

A war-built tug

around a bit to see what I could do. Mr. Sully didn't mind 'cos he got half, didn't he! Mind you, out of my half I had to pay my mate and third hand and me diesel! So you used your sails whenever you could, but on the other hand, if usin' a few gallons of diesel got you there sooner and unloaded sooner then it paid for itself several times over. Oh yes, mate, there weren't none better when it came to makin' a livin' out of an old barge! 'Cos what you could charge a merchant was all laid down in the freight rates handbook. F'r instance, wheat from London to Great Yarmouth in 1961 was 14s.10d. (74p) per ton, same for peas, lentils or maize - in bags that is. If it was loose you got 3s.1d. (15p) a quarter, which works out about a shillun a ton less. And if the cargo had to go to Norwich - you know, mate, up the River Yare - then you got another 3s.0d. (15p) a ton."

"Timber was measured in standards. A standard was 165 cubic feet if my mem'ry serves me c'rectly and you got £3.10s.11d. (£3.55) per standard loaded. These are 1961 prices just to give you an idea. Obviously they were less in 1946 when we started trading on the share system again and more by 1974 when I give up."

"An' o' course there were minimum charges too. In the example I've just given you - London to Yarmouth - there would have been a minimum charge of £80 from 1st April to 30th September and then £88 from 1st October to 31st March to take account of delays for bad weather, and also 'cos you reckoned to load about 10 ton less in winter.

"Now the merchant had to pay for all the dock dues and arrange for unloadin'. If we got stuck 'cos the merchant hadn't got things organised prop'ly we got paid what's known as demurrage. That worked out at 1s.6d. (7p) per ton per day delayed with a minimum charge of £4.10s. Five days excluding Sunday, were allowed for loading and unloading. Anything more that that which was the merchants fault and we got demurrage. Yes, mate, we weren't goin' to sit there gittin' bugger all 'cos an unloadin' gang hadn't turned up. We had to provide the gear for stuff to be lifted out, but o' course, as things got a bit more modernised, grabs and elevators did a lot o' the work."

"That was very important to see that stuff was loaded c'rectly; for one thing we wanted to get as much stuff in as possible, filling every little corner; and for another, we didn't want the cargo shiftin' if we hit some bad weather. I've seen that happen, mate, and that can put the fear o' God inter yer."

"Some of the stuff we took you never hear of now - like locust beans, hominy chop (kibbled maize kernels), milo sorghum - all used in animal foods. Our main cargo was grain of some sort, either in bulk or in sacks, but once or twice we got sent to the Humber for coal. That once took us three weeks to get back from there in winter! South-westerly gales kept us twiddlin' our thumbs for days on end. You can't earn much that way mate, no you can't!"

"Now I've told you about stack work haven't I? You know - loads of hay or straw up to London and muck for the fields on the return trip. There was a lot o' that trade going on in the years before the second war. Well, I helped revive it! Yes mate. I was takin' straw from Colchester to paper mills in Kent. We used Ridham Dock on the Swale; a rum old place. So my mate Gerry found out what that was like steerin' a stackie! I used to sit on top of the stack and give him directions. We had several o' them trips. 'Cos immediately after the war we were in big demand, but by 1950 life was gettin' harder what with steel motor barges bein' built, and much more transport by road. So you had to get anythin' that was goin'! We did three loads a fortnight in good weather. Mind you, we weren't bringing much back!"

"We took pit props to Ridham as well - not for coal mines - no, no, but for the pulp trade, paper makin'. There was a little narrow gauge railway at Ridham and we used to hitch a ride on it to Sittingbourne for a pint or two and to get a decent bit of meat. I'll tell you what mate, we never went short of good grub - not on any barge I ever worked on!"

"Part of a bargeman's life, mate, is gettin' ashore for a pint! There aren't many waterside pubs I've not visited. I don't mean gettin' drunk and all that - no, no, couldn't bloody afford it, mate! No, a nice pint in front of the fire, a bit of a yarn and a song. Oh, I know lots of songs and I love singin' 'em. Do you know 'The Princess Royal' mate? As far as I know that's somethin' to do with the American War of Independence. My father used to sing it."

"Oh yeah, they were always on at me to sing a song. I never played a concertina – I wish I had done - but I used to do step dancin' on a tin tray!"

"No mate, I didn't have much to complain about. We were kept busy up and down the East Coast and that was nice havin' my son with me. Around 1948 he met Eileen and got married in 1951. He stayed with me for a bit but he wanted to be home nights (I don't blame him, mate!) and in 1953 he got a job on the Ipswich Docks where he stayed 'til he retired."

" 'Cos I had to find another mate, din't I! Luck'ly old Moses came along just at the right moment. That weren't his real name o' cos - that was Walter Lawes, and he'd bin on a coaster called the *RAYCREEK*. But why don't you go and see him mate? He live near Yarmouth. He'll tell you all about me!"

Chapter 8

WALTER'S STORY

Walter Cook's bargeyard, where *DAWN* was built, nestles below Maldon's parish church

"I lived at Tolleshunt d'Arcy, in Essex, and as a boy always loved the barges. When I left school I worked at John Sadd's the timber merchants at Maldon. There were always barges up at Sadds and it wasn't long before I was recruited as mate aboard a barge called the *LESLIE WEST* under skipper 'Spike' from Strood in Kent. I knew nothing when I started, but skippers were finding it hard to get mates and would take on almost anyone with two arms and two legs. Anyway I stayed on *LESLIE WEST* for three years so I couldn't have been that bad! Then I did three trips with skipper Green on the *DAWN* and a few trips on the *REPERTOR* with skipper Hamilton. Even then I could see that the days of the sailing barge were coming to an end and not wanting to get left behind I joined a steel coaster called *RAYCREEK*. It was all East Coast stuff - I went to Middlesborough twice - but I yearned to be back on the barges. So when a vacancy came up on *BEATRICE MAUD* I jumped at it."

"The barge was painted battleship grey when I joined; perhaps Harold had got some Navy paint on the cheap! I felt comfortable straight away. I got on very well with Harold who for some unknown reason called me Moses! Harold loved his grub and we both took a turn at cooking. The thing about Harold was he used to learn you properly so there was no excuse, unlike one or two skippers I won't mention. We did a lot of work for Gibbons flour mill at Ipswich and also for Lee Barber's at Yarmouth - they made animal feeding stuffs. The barge could load 160 tons of grain or groundnut cake or fish meal - a bit less in winter - and we made a decent living between us."

"I only met Mr. Sully once - the owner of the barge. But most of the time it was almost as if Harold owned the barge himself! He was always looking for a return cargo and chasing up dockers to get us unloaded. He could do anything aboard a barge - splice wire, mend fenders, service the engine - anything. Sullys had four or five other barges at the time I seem to remember, *OXYGEN*, *HYDROGEN*, *RAYBEL*, *CONVOY*, the *PHOENICIAN* perhaps, and an iron-pot coaster called *PETER ROBIN*. We used to see the other barges from time to time and there was always a bit of healthy competition. By the time I joined, the barge only had the stumpy mainmast - no topmast - but we could set a mains'l and fores'l if we wanted to."

"He had some nice little touches did Harold. Like his P.L.A. (Port of London Authority) mug, he said stood for Please Leave Alone! And he was always singing sea shanties and barging songs. Here's one of his little verses I liked:

> High water London Bridge
> Half Ebb Swin
> Low Water Yarmouth
> Half flood Lynn

And of course he always had his dog with him - a sort of Jack Russell type terrier. The amazing thing is the dog would spot the buoys long before we could and start barking! Very useful at times, although to tell the truth Harold knew exactly where we were. He didn't need a chart anywhere between Ramsgate and Yarmouth."

A 'stumpy' mainmast

The King's Staithe, at Lynn

"Harold was a very gentle man - most of the time, but he could be roused! I remember once when a tug hit us in the Thames. Cor blimey! I had to hold my hands over my ears whilst Harold blasted off! Mind you, I think Harold got his own back that night when he sculled across to the tug, which was unmanned for the night, and siphoned off some cans of diesel! 'Serve the buggers bloody well right!' Harold would have said in defence."

"Other times Harold got a bit noisy was when we were coming in somewhere and he wanted someone to take a line or some other boat was in the spot he thought we should have had; there was often a bit of shouting and swearing then - but he usually had a twinkle in his eye when he was doing it."

"Anyway, the inevitable happened when on one trip to Yarmouth I fell in love with my wife to be. She loved Harold as much as I did - she used to call him Uncle! Before long we decided to get married and I didn't want to be away from home. So it was goodbye Harold, goodbye barges, and hello to a job at Birdseye Frozen Foods, after about 11 years aboard the *BEATRICE MAUD*. They were wonderful years; a great education for me and a chance to work alongside one of the best, in every respect."

Chapter 9

RACING

Bargemen not only made a living out of barges, they sometimes took their leisure in them as well. Until the start of the Second World War, barge matches took place throughout the season from the south to the north of the Thames Estuary. One or two barge owners kept a barge just for racing, never to be stressed or strained by the everyday business of carrying cargo! The barge *VERONICA*, for example, was maintained by F. T. Everard and Sons for a number of years, solely for the annual barge matches.

Harold was not the most famous of the racing sailormen, but he took his fair share of prizes. "My main claim to fame" says Harold, "was winning the Coronation Cup in the Auxiliary Class in the combined Thames and Medway race on 21st May 1953. The barge was the *EDITH MAY* and my good old friend Chubb Horlock was skipper. We

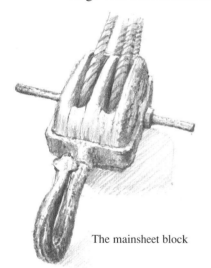

The mainsheet block

were only a total crew of four and we had to remove the propeller from the shaft to reduce drag. I seem to remember we had a bit of ballast up for'ard to balance up the weight of the engine."

"I've got a note of all the barges out that day, mate. There were three classes; the Champion Bowsprits, the Restricted Stays'ls and the Auxiliaries. In the Bowsprits there was *SARA*, *SIRDAR*, *XYLONITE* and *NELSON*. In the restricted class we had *WESTMORELAND*, *REVIVAL*, *DREADNOUGHT*, *ESTHER*, and *CLARA*. In our class - the Auxiliaries - there was *DAWN*, *WATER LILY*, *GLENMORE*, and *EDITH MAY*, owned by the guv'nor, Mr. Sully."

"The start was at nine o'clock at Hope Point but there was very little wind. The tide was a ebbin' so we had to make sure we didn't get down there too soon and cross the line ahead of time, 'cos we would have never been able to get back to the start with no wind - see what I mean, mate?"

"Anyway, as it happened we were fifth across the line at about 9.15 - not too bad. Some of the others were a long way back. The course was along the north side of the river to the Chapman light off Canvey, then down to Southend where the motor vessel *ROYAL SOVEREIGN* was being used as a mark boat. All we got was a very light easterly breeze, but we rounded the mark at about 1 o'clock, at which point the wind dropped completely! Funnily enough we could see the *SARA*, way up river, close hauled - so she'd got some wind with some west in it."

"Anyway, we 'ventually got some nice little puffs from the sou'west and we were away! 'Parently *SARA* lost a man overboard in the Lower Hope, turned round, picked him up, and still went on to win overall by miles! We went on to win the auxiliary class with *DAWN* second and *GLENMORE* third, despite a broken topmast. *WATER LILY* hit the mark boat and was disqualified. I reckon the wind dropped at a crucial point and she drifted on. *ESTHER* won the restricted class. We all got a silver medal and a pewter tankard and Mr. Sully was generous to us as well!"

A barge match

" 'Cos, I never expected barge racin' to get goin' again after the war, so it was a real privilege to be in the Coronation Cup. The number of barges tradin' was falling fast. Some were having a decent sized engine installed and losing most of their spars. Then the enthusiastic amateurs and clubs started buyin' up old barges. Sometimes an old barge with a leaky hull only fit for the scrap-heap would have some half decent spars, rigging and sails in her and some bloke with a reasonable hull, but no rigging, could do a deal and get himself a nice little number. Lots of 'em did that. Old Jack Spitty used to take *EDITH MAY* for Vernon Harvey - a farmer. Jack must have been nearly 80. He became landlord of the Goldhanger Chequers when he gave up bargin' and his mate Johnny Eve wasn't much younger. But they could sail that barge like a bloody dream - all done with nods and winks, no shoutin' nor nothin'. In the 1962 Pin Mill match, *EDITH MAY* was in a collision; I can't remember who with though. Just before the collision one of the guests on board had gone down below to the toilet, which was in the port quarter, aft. And that's where she got 'it. Christ Almighty! By all accounts that bloke shot up them steps like a bloody Jack-in-the-box - white as a sheet with his trousers half down! That must have been one hell of a shock - dear oh dear ... I'd have loved to have been there!"

"Most of my racing has been done in the *ENA* - not the fastest of barges, but I know every little scrap of tide and every little eddy in the Orwell, Stour and the harbour (Harwich). Oh yes, mate, there ain't none better! I've raced the *ENA* at Southend, Gravesend, Maldon, Brightlingsea and, of course, on the Orwell. One Saturday, I won five cups - first over the line; first around the outer mark; first back home; first in the class, and the Seamanship Cup for a good gybe round the outer mark. That was a bloody good day out, mate - especially as the Seamanship Cup had £25 in it! Mind you, you have to have a good crew! That day I had George Potter, George Waines, Micky Ducker, and Jack Southgate, the Foreman on Paul's shipyard."

Chapter 10

SWALLOWING THE ANCHOR

"Well mate, I started off in barges when I was fourteen and now I'm seventy! That's 1972 we're talkin' about now, and I've been on the water for fifty-six years - not a bad old innings, although I've known some that have worked longer - not many though. My wife was ill with cancer and Mr. Sully was less and less inclined to do the repairs and maintenance that I wanted. The days of the old barges were comin' to an end and Mr. Sully weren't one to throw good money after bad. You couldn't blame him."

"Well, we had loaded gunpowder in the Medway and were on our way to Marchwood, near Southampton, when we sprung a bad leak off Shoreham. We kept a goin' though and delivered our cargo without too much damage bein' done. I phoned Mr. Sully and he said 'Can you get her back home?' Well, I said I could, 'cos with the load out of her, the leak wasn't quite as bad. But I'd made up my mind. That was my last trip. I'd 'ad enough."

"The old barge got back to Maldon and I packed me bags. I was needed at home, really. Soon after, Mr. Sully phoned me at home. He'd sold *BEATRICE MAUD* to a couple of teachers who were going to convert her into a floating home, and would I show them the ropes. Well yes, I would, I said - but I only stayed half a day. They fell out with me and I fell out with them! They knew more about it than I did! So I left them to bloody well sort it out for themselves. I believe the old ship finally finished up at Morwellham Quay Museum in Cornwall, but from what I heard in about 1995 she was more or less fallin' to bits. A good old barge though. She kept me safe and sound and put a pound or two in me pocket as well!"

The Dock End Shipyard

"My poor wife died on 29th March 1973 in Ipswich Hospital. I'm glad I was at home for the last few months of her life. She never thought about herself. Always worryin' about the children, grandchildren, neighbours, animals and, yes mate - even me! 'Cos, she was a year or two older than me."

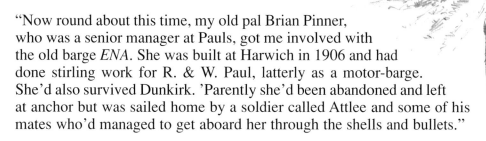
Off to work at 85

"Now round about this time, my old pal Brian Pinner, who was a senior manager at Pauls, got me involved with the old barge *ENA*. She was built at Harwich in 1906 and had done stirling work for R. & W. Paul, latterly as a motor-barge. She'd also survived Dunkirk. 'Parently she'd been abandoned and left at anchor but was sailed home by a soldier called Attlee and some of his mates who'd managed to get aboard her through the shells and bullets."

"Anyway, Pauls were going to get shot of the *ENA*, but Brian Pinner persuaded them to hold on to her, re-rig her, and use her for the benefit of the staff. Well, they agreed to that, and Charlie Webb and me re-rigged her. They couldn't have chose a better pair, mate. What we didn't know about barges weren't worth knowin'! Mind you, the first time we took her for a sail tempers got a bit frayed. We were in the Stour and I wanted some sails takin' in. I shouted at Charlie to get on with it but the silly old bugger had dropped anchor! 'Do what you bloody well like with your end,' he shouted 'mine's anchored!' We used to laugh about it afterwards. I skippered the *ENA* for several years but my sight was getting bad, so Len Polly took over and, later on, his brother Tom. But I was always around if they needed a bit of a hand or were on holiday or somethin'. Brian Pinner reckoned I was the only bloke in Ipswich what could put a barge on the blocks c'rectly. You'd think that was a simple job, floating a barge onto blocks so's she'd settle down on 'em, but that takes a bit of skill, that does, mate."

"Brian and m'self took the *ENA* to Amsterdam once, but once I saw Brian was OK I went below and slept most of the way. I like to see a bit of land, m'self. Brian reckoned I was a bit scared!"

"After giving up the *ENA*, I fixed m'self up with a job at Roy Woods, the ship repairer at Dock End in Ipswich. I've already told you, haven't I, that there's not much I can't do in the way of repairs on a ship and I'm not a nine to five person - no, Sir! If there's a rush job on I don't mind how long I work. But all the time I had a bit of an urge to get on the water again. Seems funny, don't it? So I says to my son Gerry that I'm goin' to buy a yacht. 'You must be mad' 'e said, but I was determined, so in the end he agreed to help me. He knew it was a waste of time arguin' once I'd made me mind up!"

"So off we went, lookin' around the boatyards and marinas and keepin' and eye on the adverts in the local paper. It don't take long to get an idea of what's about and what you'll get for your money. I wanted a wooden boat - none of your plastic rubbish - and I knew what I was lookin' for; a nice little 26 footer in fair condition with a good engine in her."

"We were down at Woodbridge one day and my boy Gerry was gettin' a bit fed up with me, 'cos everything we'd looked at hadn't been good enough - some of 'em you could nearly shove a pen knife through the hull! Anyway we were looking at a fair little yacht when another one came up alongside, just the sort of boat I wanted. About 27 foot, nicely painted, and sittin' in the water a real treat - you know what I mean, mate."

" 'Is she for sale?' I was surprised to find that she was. Turned out that she belonged to a doctor at the hospital and that he wanted £2000 for her. We more or less did a deal on the spot and the next day I went to the building society to get my money. They wanted to give me a cheque but I said no, no, I want cash. They were not very helpful and said they needed notice and all that, but I got cash in the end after the manager intervened. I closed my account after that."

"Next weekend my boy Gerry and his boy John came with me to sail her back to Ipswich. It was a blustery old day and we left Woodbridge about an hour before high water. When we got down to Felixstowe ferry that was blowin' half a gale and the water was runnin' out of the Deben like a train. We crashed about over the bar but soon got into deeper water. Not before the grandson John had lost his breakfast over the side though! Oh dear!"

"It was a wet old ride past Felixstowe and into the harbour with a foul tide but I was pleased with the little boat and the way she handled the rough water. I was still working at Dock End, now owned by a firm called Antens, so what better place to tie up, so I could sorta keep an eye on her and do the little odd jobs that needed doin'."

"After a while I began to get itchy feet - after all, bein' on the water was something I knew somethin' about, so I said to my son Gerry, 'Boy - we're going to have a holiday; we're agoin' to Calais and up the Belgian and Dutch Coasts to Ijmuiden. Then we'll go into the canals and come out at Flushing. We'll have a good old time just like on the barge.' But Gerry was havin' none of it! 'I can't just leave my job and my family for a month to swan around Holland!' he said. 'In that case I'll go by my bloody self.' I replied, and that was the end of it".

50

"By that time I'd moved the yacht away from Dock End Shipyard, through the lock gates, and into a nice little spot just inside the dock, not far from where we'd got the old bullock out of the water years ago - me and Frank Goddard - remember mate? I started to get the boat ready for my little expedition."

"Unbeknown to me, though, was that my boy Gerry had been down to the gates and told the lockmaster not to let me out under any circumstances! You see, he worked on the dock and knew everyone, and he never thought much of the yacht idea anyway. So there I was, stuck in the dock and not even allowed out for a day on the river!"

"So I wasn't left with no choice was I mate! I gave up all thoughts of yachtin' and put the boat on the market. 'Ventually it was sold to the then harbourmaster at St. Katherine Dock (no mate, not St Katherine's - how many times do I have to tell you!) and he sent some people to sail it round. Mind you, I went with 'em to show them the ropes and all that, but we didn't get far. Off Clacton two of 'em were drunk and one of 'em was seasick, so I turned round and came back home. Bread and cheese yachtsmen, all of 'em!"

"When I was about 82 or 83 I decided to give meself a holiday. I knew a bloke who used to work on the oil rigs out of Yarmouth but had moved onto another job out in the Seychelles. He'd written to me sayin' if ever I wanted to go out there, I could. So there we were, mate - that was an invitation I couldn't refuse, so off I toddle to a travel agent in Westgate Street and they fix it all up for me. That cost a pretty packet but I'm not going to tell you how much!"

"Anyway, off we go to Heathrow - my first time in the air, I'm surprised at how much the old plane bumps about - just like a nasty chop in the Wallet! We land in Angola, in Africa, for refuelling, I suppose, and we're all told to get off and to wait in an airport building, nothin' like Heathrow, oh, dear me, no. After a while someone comes in and says that the plane cannot go on to the Seychelles because of the political situation in Angola, not the Seychelles. So here I am stuck in the middle of Africa. Some of the other people are gettin' very agitated and demanding to see a representative of the airline. Anyway, 'ventually, someone comes along and says that by way of compensation we can all go to Egypt. I weren't too happy with that but what could I do? So off we go, and learn on the way that the airline have fixed us up with a hotel and a holiday in Egypt, all on the house. Well, mate, sometimes you have to make the best of what you're given - a lifetime in barges had taught me that. In the hotel I got pally with some Americans and saw the Pyramids and the Sphinx, but blimey mate, it was hot. Unfortunately I got dehydrated and they sent me home early. Still, quite a little adventure for an old un."

"Well, I carries on at Antens for a number of years but 'ventually I'm relegated to answering the phone and making the tea. So sod that, I think. And when I'm about 86, I chuck it in altogether. One day I was ridin' home on my bike - the old dog was in the basket - and I was goin' up Orchard Street mindin' my own business when a copper shouts at me 'Oi! You're in a one way street!' 'I'm only goin' one way.' I holler back and carry on! He didn't do nothin'. They all know me round here."

"So there we are mate, that's my life. Not a lot to complain about, some good mem'ries, and a couple o' quid to keep me goin'. As long as I can get into town and see my lady friends in the Co-op and have a nice bit of meat on the table, I'm happy!"

...

Harold Smy fell ill shortly after Christmas 1996 and died in Ipswich Hospital on 26th January 1997, aged 94. He is buried in Ipswich New Cemetery with his wife, Alice.

A few months before he died I took Harold to an event at Maldon to mark the centenary of the barge *CENTAUR*. It's a wonder we got there. I mentioned in my foreword that Harold was a tactile person, emphasising points he wished to make with slaps and thumps. On the drive to Maldon down the busy A12 he grabbed my left arm which was firmly implanted on the steering wheel, and gave quite a fright to occupants of the car we were overtaking at the time! Harold knew lots of people at Maldon, and had a lovely day. When the speeches were made Harold couldn't hear a thing but was aware that the noise of talking and laughing had stopped. Suddenly, in a loud voice, Harold exclaimed 'Christ, mate, it's like bein' in a bloody church!' Needless to say, he was the man of the moment.

At his funeral Tina Turner was played, singing Simply the Best - a sentiment endorsed by everyone who knew this grand old man of the sea.

Captain Harold Smy at the
CENTAUR centenary celebrations

Abbreviations: M.N.L. - Mercantile Navy List(s); L.R.B.C. - The London & Rochester Barge Co. Ltd., later (1924) L.R.T.C. - The London & Rochester Trading Co. Ltd.

ALAN, Off. No. 112679, registered London, built Battersea 1900, 61 Reg. Tons. Dims. 82 x 20.8 x 6.6 ft. First owner Harry Keep, 90 Lower Thames Street, City, London. Sold February 1911 by auction at Gravesend to L.R.B.C., Canal Rd., Strood, Kent. Auxiliary engine installed, wheelhouse fitted, 1947. Sailing gear later removed to trade as motor-barge. Sold early 1960s for housebarge, moored Medway, derelict 2006.

ARETHUSA, Royal Navy light cruiser, built Chatham Dockyard 1913, 3,520 G.R.T., 8 Yarrow boilers, turbine engines, 30 knots; crew 318; Armament - two 6 inch guns, six 4 inch guns, 4 T.T.; flagship of the 5th Light Cruiser Squadron. Hit mine in the Sledway channel 11th February 1916. Seriously damaged and without engines, the Destroyers *LOYAL* and *LIGHTFOOT* attempted to tow her to port, but she ran onto the Cutler shoal and became a total loss. All the crew, except some ten men killed in the explosion, were taken off. The wreck claimed at least three sailing barges; the *PEGASUS* in 1919, the *SUNBEAM* (Rochester) in 1921, and the *DOMINION* in 1924.

BEATRICE MAUD, Off. No. 129112, Registered London, built by Alfred White, Sittingbourne 1910, 80 Net Registered Tons. Owners - A. White; Samuel West, Gravesend; Kent Coasters Ltd; G. F. Sully. Saw war service in the Bristol Channel, auxiliary engined 1942 (see text). Topmast removed, then as motor-barge. Sold for conversion to yacht-barge 1972 and re-rigged. Broken up 2005/6 at Landrake, River Lynher, Cornwall.

BIJOU, Off. No. 122971, Registered London, built by R. & W. Paul, Ipswich 1906 as *ENA*, Registered Ipswich, re-named *GRAVELINES II*, Registered London 1906; re-named *BIJOU* when returned to R. & W. Paul's ownership from Dunkirk based P. Verheyden; 79 Net Registered Tons. Dims. 89.0 x 21.6 x 6.75 ft. Owner - R. & W. Paul of Ipswich. Caught fire following incendiary bombing whilst alongside quay at Mistley 3rd July 1940. Drifted onto mud flat opposite quay and burnt out. Remains visible 2006.

CLARA, Off. No. 105829, Registered London, built by Alfred White, Sittingbourne 1896, 60 Net Registered Tons. Flush-decked aft. Owners - Prior; Carter; Ellis; Francis & Gilders, Colchester. Sold to Richard S. Banyard, Little Totham, Maldon (later known as 'Dingle' Dick after purchasing the 'beetle' barge of that name). Converted to auxiliary. Stranded across Leigh Creek 1962, un-rigged hull lay on Norton's bargeyard, Charlton, before being sold and towed away above bridges. Broken up.

CONVOY, Off. No. 105557, Registered Dover, built by G. & T. Smith, Rye 1900, 73 Net Registered Tons. Dims. 88.2 x 20.8 x 6.8 ft. Owners - Crundle; A. Wife; Hempstead; M.N.L. 1957 Jane Isabel Sully, Chertsey, Surrey, managing owner, trading under G. F. Sully flag. Converted to twin-screw motor-barge, to Admiralty design with bridge above wheelhouse, 1944. Sunk when motor-barge Gt. Yarmouth Haven, Capt. George Eastland. Salved, continued trading. Sold out of trade as Constructive Total Loss following sinking in London dock, 1967, to Capt. Richard Duke; repaired and re-rigged at Pin Mill as yacht-barge. Sailed around Britain during late 1960s. Various further owners until static 'venue' moored Thames outside Ship public house, Wandsworth 1984. Remained there until broken up in 2004.

CRYALLS, Off. No. 58507, Registered Rochester, built by R. M. Shrubsall, Milton next Sittingbourne 1870, 38 Net Tons. Owners - M.N.L. 1883-1897 John Seager, Borden, Kent; M.N.L. 1901 Frank Seager, Upchurch, Kent; M.N.L. 1917 William C. Dines, 104 High St., Grays. Foundered Thames Estuary 1921, salved and sold to Willie J. Rogers, 13 Great Whip St., Ipswich. Hulked at Town Hard, Walton; possibly broken-up Pin Mill 1936.

DAWN, Off. No. 105902, Registered Maldon, built by Cook and Woodward, The Hythe, Maldon 1897, as 'stack' barge, 54 tons, for James Keeble. Sold to Francis & Gilders, Colchester. Auxiliary engine installed 1949. Later, gear removed to trade as motor-barge until sold 1964 to Brown & Son, Chelmsford, for lightering on the River Blackwater, based Heybridge Basin. Sold 1965 to Gordon Swift and re-rigged as yacht-barge. Purchased by London Borough of Newham as community services vessel; laid-up in disrepair 1991. Restoration (rebuild) being undertaken by trust established for purpose with substantial funding from private and local sources plus majority Heritage Lottery Funding. Expected back in commission 2007.

DORIS, Off. No. 113759, Registered Ipswich, built by R. & W. Paul, Ipswich 1904, 62 Tons. Dims. 84 x 20 x 6 ft. Owner - R. & W. Paul of Ipswich. Mined on tow from Dunkirk, 1st June 1940, abandoned.

DREADNOUGHT, Off. No. 123849, Registered London, built by Alfred White, Sittingbourne 1907, 70 Net Registered Tons. Dims. 87.1 x 20.5 x 6.5 ft. Owners - E. J. & W. Goldsmith; T. F. Wood 1947; I.C.I. 1954; Cattedown Wharves (F. T. Everard & Sons Ltd.) 1957, for whom she became a successful racing barge. Broken up at Greenhithe shortly after the 1963 Centenary Thames Match.

EAST ANGLIA, Off. No. 127252, Registered Rochester, built by Gill, Rochester 1908, 46 Net Registered Tons. Dims. 82.9 x 17.5 x 5.4 ft. Owner - L.R.B.C., Canal Rd., Strood, Kent. Sunk in collision with S.B. *GLENWAY* in 1948. Used as mooring barge hulk, moored off Denton, painted/tarred (?) all over except dark green transom. Hulked Whitewall Creek, no trace remaining.

EDITH MAY, Off. No. 116180, Registered Harwich, built by J. & H. Cann, Harwich, launched 13th February 1906, 64 Net Tons. Dims. 86.5 x 20.0 x 6.3 ft. Net Tonnage reduced to 54 on installation of auxiliary engine. Owners - W. T. Bagrey; Barrett; G. F. Sully. Auxiliary 1952, raced in Coronation Barge Match 1953, then converted to motor-barge. Sold for conversion to yacht-barge 1961, owner Vernon Harvey. Various owners until based Liverpool Docks in maritime museum, returned to 'home' waters 1990. Undergoing extensive rebuild at Lower Halstow, Kent, by current owner Geoffrey Gransden.

ELDRED WATKINS, Off. No. 109210, Registered Ipswich, built by Orvis, Ipswich 1901, 54 Net Registered Tons. Dims. 84 x 20.2 x 5.6 ft. Owner - Albert Watkins, Ipswich, and named after his father. Sunk by steamship, River Orwell, salved, sold to F. W. Horlock, Mistley. Repaired by Mistley Shipbuilding Co. and renamed *REVIVAL*, continued trading under sail. Sold 1938 to T. F. Wood Successors for Thames explosives trade, later becoming I.C.I. One of eight sailing barges engaged in the explosives trade based at Denton. Sold 1957 to Darling Bros. Ltd. , converted to motor-barge for same work. Sold out of trade and re-rigged as barge-yacht. Still afloat and owned in France 2005 at museum, undergoing restoration.

EMILY, Off. No. 86613, Registered Ipswich, built by W. Bayley, Ipswich 1882, 57 Tons. Leeboards worked by tackles, originally tiller steered. Owner - R. & W. Paul, Ipswich. Sold to Brown & Son, Chelmsford, 1949, for use as timber lighter on River Blackwater. Hulked Woolverstone, River Orwell; burnt 1978.

ENA, Off. No. 122974, Registered Ipswich, built by McLearon, Harwich 1906, 73 Tons. Owner - R. & W. Paul, Ipswich. Auxiliary engined 1949, becoming motor-barge. Re-rigged by owners in 1973 as Company yacht-barge for staff use. Believed sold to private buyer late 1990s. Still in commission 2006.

ESTHER, Off. No. 104945, Registered Faversham, built by Alfred Marconi White, Faversham 1900, 43 Net Registered Tons. Dims. 81.3 x 18.6 x 5.3 ft. Re-measured 47 Net Tons on installation of engine 1953. Owners - Seager, Faversham; Horsford (brick makers), Faversham; M.N.L. 1957 Frederick Cremer, managing owner, Tankerton, Kent. Raced just once, in the 1953 Coronation Barge Match, winning her class. She was then engined and sold to Daniels Bros. (Whitstable) Limited, for whom she traded until 1960, the last two years as a subsidiary of L.R.T.C.. Became a housebarge at Wouldham, River Medway. Hulked West Hoo Creek.

GIPPING, Off. No. 97676, Registered Ipswich, built by Peck, Ipswich 1889, 59 Tons. Dims. 80.3 x 18.5 x 5.9 ft. Originally tiller steered. Owners - R. & W. Paul of Ipswich; T. F. Wood Successors, later becoming I.C.I., for Thames explosives trade. Sold to John & June Prime, Maldon, and converted to yacht-barge, hulked Pin Mill 1980s.

GLENMORE, Off. No. 113710, Registered Rochester, built by Little, Rochester 1902, 61 Tons. dimensions - 85.0 x 20.5 x 6.7 ft. Flush-decked aft. Net Tonnage reduced to 53 on installation of auxiliary engine. Owners - Little; W. R. Cunis, mainly in the Colne to London sand and ballast trade. Topmast later removed. Last trading barge to carry company colours - red & white - on sprit bands. Sold to War Department which renamed her H.M.S. *GLENMORISTON*. Engined 1942; un-rigged hull laid-up at Charlton before broken up c.1956.

GRAVELINES I, Off. No. 120785, Registered London, re-Registered Ipswich 1912, built by R. & W. Paul, Ipswich 1905 as *HILDA*, Registered Ipswich, 77 Net Registered Tons. Dims. 86.5 x 21.6 x 6.75 ft. Owner - R. & W. Paul of Ipswich. Auxiliary engine installed 1949, later trading as motor-barge with foresail and trisail. Sails removed to trade as pure motor-barge. Owning company renamed Paul's Foods. Sunk in collision whilst on passage near the Ovens buoy in the Thames estuary 16th June 1965. Raised and declared Constructive Total Loss and abandoned, beached at Denton. Part burned 1971.

GRAVELINES II, see *BIJOU*.

HYDROGEN, Off. No. 123640, Registered London 12th May 1906, built by Gill and Sons, Chatham Intra yard, Rochester, 98 Net Registered Tons. Originally built with 'tar' tanks, loaded 200 tons to sea. Mule-rigged spritsail barge, carried mizzen topsail. First owner Burt, Boulton & Heywood Ltd., Cannon St, City, London. Sold 9th August 1912 to George Andrews, Borden, Sittingbourne, tanks removed, converted for dry cargo work. Sold to G. F. Sully, auxiliary engine installed 1940, net tonnage reduced to 88, mizzen removed, wheelhouse fitted. February 1941 voyaged Tilbury to Greenock on war service, returned November 1945, overhauled and continued trading. Sailing gear later reduced to mainsail and foresail, sails later removed to trade as motor-barge, last wooden ex. sailing barge to trade. Sold 1979 to Bell's Whisky for promotion work, re-rigged Maldon, now owned by Topsail Charters. Still in commission under sail 2006.

KATHLEEN, Off. No. 113708, Registered Rochester, built by Lewis Glover, Gravesend 1901, 59 Tons. Dims. 82.8 x 19.7 x 6.0 ft. Re-measured 53 Tons when Kelvin 66 K3 installed 1946. Owner - Arthur Glover & William Duttson; 1909 Whitstable Shipping Company; 1916 Daniels Bros. (Whitstable) Limited, bought by L.R.T.C. in 1958. Sold for lightering to Brown & Son, Chelmsford 1961. Sold to Richard Walsh in 1966 for conversion to yacht-barge, derelict Spaarndam, Holland, by 1994. Broken up.

LANDFIELD, Off. No. 50175, Registered London, built Grays 1864, 52 Net Tons (later 45). First owner William Leonard Landfield, Grays; M.N.L. 1892 Samuel Lequire, Pier Wharf, Grays (Managing Owner), M.N.L. 1895 - 1901 George Edgar Underwood, Southend. Sold to William Bowman, Southend. M.N.L.1917 - 1920 Samuel West Ltd, 40 Trinity Square, City, London; M.N.L. 1925 William Rogers, Ipswich Malting Company (re-registered Ipswich); M.N.L. 1927-1933 William Smy, 36 Suffolk Rd., Ipswich (Managing Owner). Derelict Fagbury, River Orwell, before WWII. Remains of *LANDFIELD* and *ALASKA* buried under Felixstowe Dock extension 1974.

LESLIE WEST, Off. No. 112762, Registered London, built by Lewis Glover, Gravesend 1900, 57 Tons. Similar barge to *KATHLEEN* and *THE BROWNIE*. Owner - Samuel West Limited, London. Last trading for Francis & Gilders, Hythe Quay, Colchester. Sold for lightering to Sadds, Maldon, 1963. Abandoned Heybridge Creek. Purchased for re-rigging by Richard Duke, towed to Pin Mill 1967, where re-rigging abandoned and converted to housebarge. Derelict by 1995. Broken up 2004.

MARY ANN, Off. No. 21345, Registered Harwich, built Ipswich 1859, 54 Net Registered Tons. Dims. 75.2 x 17.1 x 5.8 ft. Bow-rail names carved on banners with short flagstaff. Owners - M.N.L. 1865 John Watt Jnr., Harwich; M.N.L. 1883 William Went, Harwich; M.N.L. 1892 Robert Peck, Dock End Ship Yard, Ipswich. Tonnage re-measured at 46 Net Tons. M.N.L. 1895-1933 Thomas S. Damant, 4 Burlington Rd., Ipswich; 1937 Paine (?). Hulked as breakwater with other elderly barge hulls at Pattricks Dock - Dovercourt Sailing Club. Registry not closed until September 1953.

NELSON, Off. No. 120590, Registered London, built by Alfred White, Sittingbourne 1905, 63 Net Registered Tons. Dimensions - 86 x 20.1 x 5.5 ft. Owners - A. & R. Sales; S. J. Brice 1932; Eastwoods until 1953; S. J. Brice; Allsworth. Hulked Queenborough, remains burnt Shepherds Creek c.1970.

OXYGEN, Off. No. 104329, Registered Rochester, built by Gill, Rochester 1895, rebuilt 1926, 69 Net Registered Tons. Owners - Burt, Boulton & Heywood; Bates; Smeed Dean, later Associated Portland Cement Manufacturers (A.P.C.M.); Sully; Horlock; Arthur Jemmett; Brown. Auxiliary by 1947; one time tar tank-barge. Housebarge Chambers Dock, Faversham 1987. Moved to Maldon, Essex for rebuilding; project abandoned 1993, hulked in Back Channel, Maldon by 1995.

P.1., (Dumb lighter) Off. No. 131226, Registered Kings Lynn, built Wivenhoe 1915, 303 Net Registered Tons. Owner - R. & W. Paul Limited, Ipswich. Towed astern of Paul's steamboats on coastal voyages, carried trisails on three masts. Later used as lighter and storage barge in Ipswich Dock. Sold abroad.

PETER ROBIN (EX. MARDY), Registered and owned Kings Lynn (1930), built of steel at Dalmuir, 1916, as 'Dardanelles' landing craft ('Beetle Barge') 108 Net Registered Tons, 156 Gross Tons. Sold to G. F. Sully, London, barge owner. Broken up by Thomas Ward, Grays.

PHOENICIAN, Off. No. 146700, Registered London, built by Wills & Packham, Sittingbourne 1922, 81 Net Registered Tons. Dims. 84.1 x 20.8 x 7.3 ft. Owners - A. Horlock; 1927 M.N.L. Alfred Sully, managing owner; later Bernard Sully, trading as G. F. Sully, barge owners. Damaged by fire alongside Marriage's Mill, Felixstowe Dock, during WWII. Moored on foreshore up-river with only mainmast standing. Later towed to Sittingbourne and by 1949 hull 'doubled' and converted to twin-screw motor-barge. Sold out of trade to A. Groom and re-rigged as yacht-barge, later purchased by Grant Littler. Still in commission under sail 2006.

RAVEN, Off. No. 118213, Registered Rochester, built by Gill, Rochester 1904, 46 Net Registered Tons. Dims. 79.9 x 17.6 x 5.8 ft. Re-measured 41 Tons when converted to motor-barge and Kelvin 44 K2 installed 1950. Owner - L.R.B.C., Canal Rd., Strood, Kent. Built to trade on charter to East Mills, Colchester. Sold c.1965 to private owner - house barge Battersea and Chiswick. Sold, towed to Maldon February 1976. Later sold and moored Flag Creek near Brightlingsea. Sold as supposed 'attraction' at East Mills. Broken up below the Mill - remains visible 2006.

RAYBEL, Off. No. 145058, Registered London, built by Wills & Packham, Sittingbourne 1920, 80 Net Registered Tons. Dims. 86.7 x 21.4 x 6.5 ft. Original owner - Alfred Sully, managing owner, named after son Raymond and mother Isabel, M.N.L. 1957 Mrs Jane Isabel Sully, trading under G. F. Sully flag. Auxiliary from 1939, then motor-barge. Sold out of trade and re-rigged as yacht-barge/studio. Still afloat and rigged 2006.

RAYCREEK (EX. KUBO), Registered London (1935), built of steel at Delfzijl, Holland, 1932, 91 Net Registered Tons, 181 Gross Tons. Owned by Samuel West, London, barge owners; R. Lapthorn & Co. Ltd., Buttercrock Wharf, Hoo, Kent, shipowners.

REPERTOR, Off. No. 145404, Registered Harwich, built of steel by Horlock, Mistley 1924, 69 Net Tons. Owners - F. W. Horlock, then M. F. Horlock, Mistley. Under-powered auxiliary engine installed 1956 - later converted to twin-screw tank-barge trading Silvertown to Queenborough, Kent and Brantham, Suffolk for B. X. Plastics. Replaced by Dutch-built vessel renamed *REPERTOR II*. Re-rigged as yacht-barge by Graham Reeve. Sold to Charles McLaren, then David Pollock 1987. Still in commission under sail 2006.

ROYAL SOVEREIGN, built of steel at Dumbarton 1948, as excursion passenger vessel.

SARA, Off. No. 115858, Registered London, built by Alfred Marconi White, Conyer (Teynham), Kent 1902, 50 Net Registered Tons. Dims. 84.6 x 18.9 x 5.8 ft. Owners - S. H. Horlock, Mistley 1903; A. H. Horlock, Mistley 1905; F. T. Everard & Sons Ltd. 1929, for whom she became a very successful racing barge. Broken up at Greenhithe shortly after the 1963 Centenary Thames Match.

SHEAF GARTH, Registered Newcastle, built Blyth 1921. Owner - Sheaf Steam Shipping Company Limited, Newcastle-on-Tyne. (Owned 9 steamships and 1 motorship in 1933 M.N. List.)

SIRDAR, Off. No. 110033, Registered London, built by Shrubsall, Ipswich 1898, 53 Net Registered Tons. Owners - Shrubsall; Owen Parry; L.R.T.C.. Kept as sailing barge for barge matches and as company 'yacht'. Successful in barge match rivalry with Everard barges. Auxiliary engine installed 1963, Net Tonnage reduced to 29 when converted for promotional work. Undertook Bell's Scotch Whisky charter in 1966 sailing London, South Coast, Belgium, Holland under Capt. Tom Baker, mate Barry Pearce. Hulked at Bedlams Bottom, Kent.

SPERANZA, Off. No. 110054, Registered London, built of steel by Fay, Southampton 1899, 67 Net Registered Tons. Owner - E. J. & W. Goldsmith Limited, 110 Fenchurch Street, City, London; L.R.T.C.. Used as lighter from 1951, broken up c.1954. Charles Lambert, known as Gentleman Charlie, murdered aboard in November 1931, aged 57.

THE SISTERS, Off. No. 45644, registered Maldon, built of iron at Blackwall 1863, 33 net tons. Dims. 69.7 x 14.4 x 4.3 ft. Built for Thomas Ward, miller at Beeleigh. Owners - M.N.L.s 1865 Henry Ward, Beeleigh (Beeleigh Mill burnt down 1875 - site abandoned by miller Henry Ward); 1883-5 Alfred Warren, Fullbridge House, Maldon (corn merchant); 1887-1892 Edward Herbert Humphreys, Maldon (managing owner) (corn merchant); 1892-1911 Eugene Wells, Buxhall Vale, Stowmarket, Suffolk, (managing owner). 31st January 1913, sailed from Felixstowe for Rochester with barley screenings - foundered E. Spile - skipper and mate took to boat and made Mouse Lightvessel.

THREE SISTERS, Off. No. 50454, Registered Maldon, built by William Smee, Shipowner of Maldon, for own use, but he died during construction in 1864. Launched 14th February 1865, 43 (originally 47) tons. Dims. 72.4 x 18.3 x 4.9 ft. Smee's widow Lucy became owner. Sold to James Richard Smee of Maldon 1876. Sold to Joseph Sadler, sailmaker, The Hythe, Maldon 1885 Owners - M.N.L. 1885-1901, George Miller, Alpha Cottage, Albemarle St., Harwich; M.N.L. 1917, ditto at 12 Third Ave., Dovercourt; M.N.L. 1919 - 1927, George R. Fulcher, 4 Salisbury Rd., Ipswich; Hulked late 1920s Kirton Creek, River Deben - remains visible 2006.

VERONICA, Off. No. 120691, Registered London, built by Horace Shrubsall, East Greenwich 1906, 54 Net Registered Tons. Dimensions - 85 x 19.2 x 5.9 ft. Owners - Clement Parker, Bradwell, Essex; V. H. Parker; F. T. Everard & Sons Ltd., Greenhithe 1932, for whom she became arguably the most successful racing barge ever. Sold as housebarge c.1963, name changed to *VERONICA BELLE*; hulked at Bedlams Bottom, Kent.

WATER LILY, Off. No. 114334, Registered London, built by Gill & Son, Rochester 1902, 58 Net Registered Tons. Dims. 83.0 x 20.0 x 6.0 ft. Re-measured 48 Tons when Kelvin 66 K3 installed 1948. Owners - J. Spitty; Clement Parker; Wakeley Bros 1933; I.C.I.; Darling Bros. Auxiliary by 1949, then converted to motor-barge, sold for housebarge in 1970s, but never converted; fell into disrepair at Pin Mill where a hulk by 1986. Broken up.

WAVENEY, Off. No. 97685, Registered Ipswich, built by Peck, Ipswich 1892, 49 Tons. Owner - R. & W. Paul of Ipswich. Sold 1933 for conversion to yacht-barge, based at Conyer until early 1960s, derelict Chichester Harbour by 1964 - burnt.

WESTMORELAND, Off. No. 112733, Registered London, built by Alfred White, Conyer 1900, 43 Net Registered Tons. Dims. 79.0 x 17.1 x 5 ft. Owners - Eastwoods (brick makers); one of their 'County' named series of barges. Acquired out of trade by the Thames Barge Sailing Club. Wrecked following high tide stranding on concrete lighter at Hoo 1973. Ownership passed to Colin Frake at Faversham, where now lying. Some repair work undertaken, but project seemingly abandoned.

WINIFRED, Off. No. 98328, registered Colchester, built by H. Felton, Sandwich 1893, 66 Registered Tons. First owners W. Felton & Partners, Sandwich; sold 1895 to William W. Tritton, Stone St, Faversham (Managing Owner); sold 1916 to L.R.B.C., Canal Rd., Strood, Kent. Sold 1946 after weather damage to private owner as barge-yacht. Engined, sailing gear removed, wheelhouse fitted. 10th September 1956 on voyage Grays to Flushing, towed to Margate leaking and beached. Later moored in harbour and pumped out by fire brigade. 22nd September 1956 stranded on West Barrow Sand, filled and broke up.

XYLONITE, Off. No. 145408, Launched as *B.X.*, Registered Harwich, immediately re-named *XYLONITE*, built of steel by Mistley Shipbuilding (Horlock), Mistley 1926, 68 Net Tons. Owners - F. W. Horlock; Tester, as motor-barge. Re-rigged as charter barge by Tim Elliff. Sold 1986 to Cirdan Trust for community service. Still in commission under sail 2006.